21 + 1

21 + 1
THE FORTUNE-TELLER'S RULES

READ LIKE THE DEVIL MANIFESTOS

EDITED BY CAMELIA ELIAS

EYECORNER PRESS

21+1: THE FORTUNE–TELLER'S RULES
READ LIKE THE DEVIL MANIFESTOS

Published by EYECORNER PRESS | DIVINATION SERIES
September 2018, Thy, Denmark

ISBN: 978-87-92633-41-5

Cover design, layout and editorial by Camelia Elias.
Typeset in Euphemia UCAS and Krungthep.

All images in this book are based on art created by the individual authors, contributors to this book. They are used here by their kind permission.

Printed in the UK and US.

FOR THE STUDENTS
WHO LISTEN

Contents

Illustrators

The Fortune-Teller's Cut
An Introduction

Camelia Elias

'I wonder if they listen,' I ask myself not, when I teach a cartomancy class.

What I do instead is make a call for contributions to a book of principles and precepts.

I give people a template and a few examples of what I'm looking for, and then say: 'Go. Show me what you've learnt. Show me how you draw, cut, and sheathe. Show me how you read the damn cards. Show me how you read like the Devil.'

The idea of cartomantic precepts is inspired by my life-long interest in martial arts where discipline and a deep understanding of core principles rule.

I've been referring to my teaching and practice as 'martial arts cartomancy', insofar as what I have to say is anchored in operating with a set of trifecta.

For instance, the martial arts principle of 'draw, cut, and sheathe' is my exact equivalent to shuffling, cutting to the bones precisely what I see, and getting the hell out of there by putting the cards back in their case, leaving as well all self-doubt and speculation at the door. After I sheathe, I don't go: 'I wonder if my prediction will come to pass,' or 'I wonder if I'm full of shit.'

Cartomancy as rationale, not method

What you're about to experience is 37 diviners, students and associates of Aradia Academy, and their take on divination that's ruled by such principles. The instruction was that each contributor formulates a set of 22 rules that captures the essence of cartomantic practice.

The fortune-telling voices gathered here come from both reputed veteran and young cartomancers. The purpose of the blended choir is to demonstrate how progression towards wisdom is experienced and achieved in different contexts and under different conditions.

My ambition with this book is thus to display the very heart of reading cards beyond what we call 'teaching', 'instruction', 'essential keys to cartomancy' or 'the secret to fortune-telling.'

The approach to this 'beyond' is in the instruction that the fortune-teller keeps it simple, and formulates 21+1 snappy rules, delivered with martial arts aplomb in the form of manifestos.

While each fortune-teller imparts his or her own flavor and deep wisdom about what works and what doesn't in any cartomantic session, the idea is to go beyond the flashy, the verbose, and the dictatorial, and rather, suggest instead what the nerve of each individual contribution to cartomancy is all about.

As you read through each fortune-teller's rules, you will notice that quite a few keywords are shared across that highlight the teachings of Aradia Academy.

These keywords stress principles of design, movement, semiotics, and hermeneutics.

This means that while the rules cover a wide range of approaches to cartomancy and divination, they are also carefully calculated and anchored in a movement that goes from observing the cards on table and their strictly formal composition to offering perspectives on the metaphysics of interpretation.

Put differently, this book is not a textbook that tells you what to read and in what order. This is a book that asks you to think about why you see what you see. The book shoots for each fortune-teller's highest, sharpest, fastest, and most elegant wisdom. Nothing more, nothing less.

RULES WITHOUT IDENTITY

Given the title of this book, 21+1 rules, you may think that what's presented here is the blueprint, or the very identity of a fortune-teller, her essence and experience.

Indeed, while the idea is to showcase what makes a diviner, I'd have to say that since I myself am not at all fond of concepts such as identity and blueprint, as they smack of the illusion of stability, what I'm looking for instead are sharp cuts and the space between them.

You can only make a sharp cut if you watch intently what's under your nose. You also have to know how what's under your nose moves. How fast, how slow?

Many schools will teach you method and technique, but there's nothing that's more powerful than what you can learn about a situation by simply paying great attention to what's happening. Make your cuts in accordance. Then sheathe.

If you read the cards for another, how do you hear the question? What is moving in the other person's voice? How does the person you read the cards for stretch herself in telling you what's at stake in her predicament? How do you stretch your own elastic of delivering a message in relation to what you see and what you hear? Can you register your breaking point? If you can't, watch some more and listen some more.

As for the cards, do you look at the interaction between them? Or are you ready to launch into lecturing about the meaning of each individual card? This can be fascinating in and of itself, but if you want to develop virtuosity in the art of cutting, then it's not 'meanings' you'll be repeating, but rather, you'll be observing essential and subtle moves.

How do you move from the cups to the swords, from the coins to the batons?

Although we have 4 suits in a deck of cards, the movement between them is a simple 2-way understanding of what to keep and what to discard. That's what you want to know.

Martial arts cartomancy stresses looking intently at how the cards manifest what you really want to keep and what you want to discard. You pass the same principle on to the other.

What do the cards really say? Keep the love, or get rid of it? Keep the job or get rid of work? Keep the body workout, or try something new? Keep the boundaries, or take down the fences?

The numbers are there to tell you something about the degree of your actions when it comes to what to keep and what to discard.

Meanwhile, the starting point is in the question you pose to the other: 'Are you sure this is what you want to know?' That's the first draw. If heaven is with you, if the earth is with you, and if your heart is open and wise, then there's no way you're going to lose this battle.

Every divination session is a battlefield. The fortune-teller must win every time. What's the point of divining, if not to win over problems, insecurities, illusions, disappointments, sorrows, the heart's desires, and dreams?

You are not the diviner you are, because you have figured things out. You are the diviner you are, because as soon as you figure things out, you apply the process to the unknown as it presents itself to you in the form of a puzzle, often putting your newly formulated rules to shame.

CORRECT PREDICTION

This book is not yet another exercise in what happens when you join the mainstream choir and intone: 'Whatever works for you'. I see no ambition in that.

Rather, this book aims at giving you something of a clean and fresh cut, one that takes 'whatever works for you' to another level. This is the level of the intuitive as it consists of a mode of seeing things clearly.

The 21+1 rules are not aimed at extending labels, or exploring the symbolic archetype of what it means to be a fortune-teller.

The 21+1 rules dissolve the borders created in the mind of the fortune-teller – the fortune-teller as culturally defined – as 'one who professes to foretell future events'.

Instead of offering rules for how to improve your accuracy in your predictive readings, or promise to reveal some untold secret that has been well-guarded by the fortune-telling cast, the 21+1 rules take you to the place of realizing simple truths.

If you can divine and have a set of rules that you can claim are yours, because they work for you, then it's because you have managed to internalize the idea that heaven, earth, and mankind are but one concoction, separated in the conceptual only by a terrific sense of timing and of place.

Nowhere else than in the oldest book of divination we have in coherent form, the I-Ching, is this better explicitated. We may as well remember it.

The 21+1 rules are not part of an effort that will tell you how you can continue 'the tradition,' or 'the lineage.' If anything, the only thing you can dream of continuing is a method that you keep revising, not what we call 'the spirit' of this or that.

If you work from within the flow of life, from knowing momentum and restraint and when the time is right to either engage in delivering your full message or refrain from it, then you realize that 'spirit' is not something that you carry within, that you honor and promise to uphold in yet another set of rules that smacks of the illusion of stability.

Rather, you know that the spirit that drives you is informed by acknowledging the law of impermanence, and that the only prediction you can be sure to always get right is the universal one: 'You're also going to die.'

THE SWIFT AND THE SOLID CUT

Take this obvious statement: A pack of cards has four dimensions.

Imagine your 78, 52, or 36 cards, spread on your table face down. That's your data.

Now pick three cards out of the pile. They have names and images that you recognize have a specific symbolic value. That's your information.

You put two and two together, and declare: 'This means that'. That's your knowledge.

Now, you reflect: 'Why did I say that, where does that come from?' That's your wisdom.

In a way, teaching cartomancy for me is no different than teaching students to write projects at the university.

At the exam I'm not interested in hearing about the descriptive level that goes through all 4 dimensions: data, information, knowledge and wisdom.

What I'm interested in is how the students can trace back their reflection of the 'why' to the 'what' and the 'how.' That is what is called a positioning.

The movement upwards from data to wisdom is called a swift cut. The movement down from wisdom to data is called a solid cut.

What I want is a nuanced answer to the classical string of questions for investigation: What are these cards, how to they work, why do I say what I say, and for what purpose? What I want is a clear answer as to the function of the wisdom gained from having gone through internalizing the other processes.

Many new diviners on the block shoot straight for the knowledge and the wisdom of the cards and try to develop a practice based on processing their experiences. Yet not all are aware of the fact that the entire pile of cards that conveys information is anchored in context. What is this context, and why do we need to know about it?

I have collected the 21+1 rules here with view to giving others a taste of the rationale behind the fortune-teller's process of thinking and distilling significance out of the information that's put on her table.

All the contributions to this book have a pragmatic, or practical approach, though some filter this pragmatism through a poetic nerve or meta-voice that enters into dialogue with the act of divination itself.

What does it mean to divine when you lie in bed naked, drawing cards and resisting the cut: 'He loves me not?' While not sheathing may place you in a state of grace, where you look at the blood dripping from your blade, encouraging the agony of 'and yet...' – pragmatically speaking, are you still a martial artist of the cards?

This is not the book to answer this question, but you will see that the fortune-tellers' rules here all reflect a shared conviction: Apart from predicting or counseling, what we do with the cards is tell a story.

What enables the story is a context and a question. Without a context and a question there's no story that has purpose and precision, and hence, there's no divination that's worth anything. Just opinion won't cut it.

There isn't a single experienced and serious diviner I know who won't readily agree to that. In this sense, we're a school that follows these principles:

context + question + cards =
divination

context + question + cards + discipline =
martial arts divination

context + question + cards + discipline + clarity =
Zen divination

THE SCHOLARSHIP

I hope you all enjoy this ride. I bow to the wisdom of my students and the associates of Aradia Academy. They give meaning to my shifting of lanes from the university to the academy, teaching Cards and Zen to all who want to learn, and taking also the virtual encounters in the social media or via the webinars to a place of material manifestation, where we don't just talk about it, but actually do something for one another, and elevate each other's understanding.

With this publication, Aradia Academy is also instituting a scholarship, hereby called 'The 21+1 Scholarship', to be awarded to a brilliant cartomancer who has an open heart, but is short of money. Applications for this grant will be open in connection with each course on offer. Stay tuned, and, as ever, keep going.

Camelia Elias, PhD, Dr.Phil.
Director of Aradia Academy

Hemsedal, Norway
August 3, 2018

XIII by Michele Benzamin-Miki

Hol Dit

Enrique Enriquez

SHUFFLE. The tarot is not a bird, but a collection of feathers.

SHUFFLE. By holding it in our hand we grasp the reality of the object.

SHUFFLE. There is more truth in the deck itself than in all the images it contains.

SHUFFLE. The main thing a pack of cards tells us is that images come and go.

SHUFFLE. Only the shuffle is permanent.

SHUFFLE. That is the true structure of a tarot deck: The shuffle.

SHUFFLE. The cards are in a state of potential shuffle even when they rest in our pocket.

SHUFFLE. As soon as we shuffle the deck, we turn a square into a circle.

SHUFFLE. As things get in motion, they lose their sharp corners.

SHUFFLE. That is what life does to us: We start with straight ideas of what we want, and life rounds us up.

SHUFFLE. From the point of view of the table, the cards are just blocking the light.

SHUFFLE. Cards reveal as much as they occlude.

SHUFFLE. Cards are only as useful as we make them.

SHUFFLE. By placing a card on the table we lower a bridge.

SHUFFLE. Whenever we share an experience with another person we are entering a bridge from opposite sides.

SHUFFLE. Even when we think we agree in what is seen, we may be seeing something different.

SHUFFLE. No matter what we see, something joyful or dismal, as soon as we are done seeing it we will put the cards back in the deck.

SHUFFLE. Whatever we see and say will be gone, lost in the shuffle.

SHUFFLE. Oracles don't say anything about us, they show us how life works. They only talk about us as far as we are in life.

SHUFFLE. Oracles don't present us with symbols, but operate on a different symbolic order, where they resemble life in the constancy of change.

SHUFFLE. The only good reason to stop and look at the cards on the table is to beat common sense out of its own boredom.

> **SHUFFLE.** Learn the tarot very well, so you never have to use it.

*

ENRIQUE ENRIQUEZ is a tarot reader, philosopher, artist, and poet living in New York City.

Birds by Enrique Enriquez

Litany of the Bugs

Wendy Lee Gadzuk

Aim for clarity, sharp as a sword, shiny and hard as a polished diamond.

Don't let the bugs in.

Hesitation and doubt will let the bugs in.

To do something, there must be something to do. The story is already on the table. Tell it.

The glow of the Hermit's lamp does not attract the bugs, because he is wise enough to go where they are not.

Don't speak to fill the void. Let the story on the table become the void. Simply tell it.

Every card has a back.

If the Emperor can take care of business with his legs crossed, so can you. Or uncross them, if you prefer. We don't know what's going on under La Papesse's robes.

Be consistent. The bugs are opportunists.

The cards talk amongst themselves when we are not listening, tucked away. That's why they know the answer to the question before it is even asked.

The question is the prize. Eye on the prize. If we're not careful, the buzzing of the fly can become our focus. Don't let the bugs in.

The Magician knows how to distract the bugs so that he can do his work.

You are a translator. Language is important. It is the bridge between the cards and the story and the sitter. Aim to master it.

10 cups of water are good if you want to put out a fire. But all that water can attract mosquitoes.

The cards are really just identical blank rectangles with different pictures and numbers on them.

To the bugs, a King is no different than a Page. They all taste the same.

Know your enemy. It is more work for the termites to eat 10 Batons than 2.

Pay attention to who or what didn't show up in the story.

Tell the story of the cards that you see (or don't see) but not the story of each card that you see.

Learn from the past. Part of the Hermit's wisdom comes from learning as the Magician how to bend the light, beyond the bugs.

When you are done, close the door. Don't let the bugs in.

The bugs say, "Where there is nothing, we too, are nothing.

*

WENDY LEE GADZUK is a visual artist, writer, musician and diviner living and working in the Mojave Desert of California. Inspired by our universal connection to the divine, she works in various mediums, exhibiting regularly in the Los Angeles area and beyond. The work holds a similar thread, connecting in its own way to the collective unconscious, seeking its own sober truth, through words, images and sound.

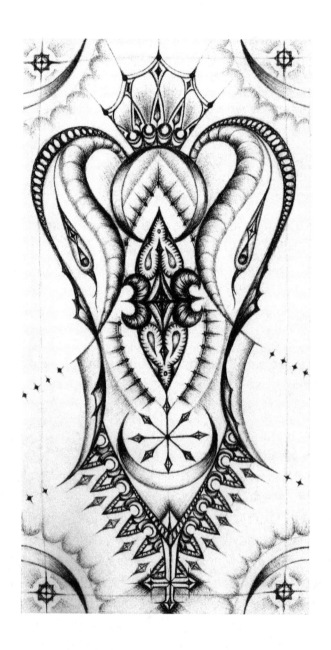

Hydra by Wendy Lee Gadzuk

Poor Reader's Almanac

Jeff Silverstein

Kings, queens, knights, and castles. Flat chess.

Find the triangles, they are strong.

Magician Dai Vernon said that a card is a very light thing and there are many ways to turn it over.

The first question is not the real question. The mind creates it to hide what you fear.

The unconscious is there to protect you from predators – and to know when you are one. Ask any animal.

Neither the reader nor the querent is playing with a full deck. That's the strength.

Don't focus on secrets somebody drew into the cards – draw your own truths out of them.

You can have power without having "powers."

Read parked cars. Flowers in a garden. Boxes of cereal on a supermarket shelf.

Tear up an entire deck one card at a time. That will remind you who's boss.

Some answers float above the cards. Some are underneath. Some are on the edges.

You will see the hero immediately. The villain may hide. Ask what each one wants.

Many writers fling characters onto the page and wait to see what they say and do. Wait.

If the cards don't make sense, explain why they don't – that's actually the answer.

When you get confused, squint at the cards – a bright spot will point to clarity.

Grip the cards too tightly and their voice is muffled.

Animate the pips in your mind. Don't count them – see them move and transform.

If even a few notes of a song go through your mind during a reading, listen.

They dreamt about their question last night and will dream about your answer tonight.

The Visconti–Sforza Hermit is Time. Use his hourglass.

Sometimes Einstein rides his bicycle around the cards. There he is now.

The deck says: "I was once a tree."

*

JEFF SILVERSTEIN is a screenwriter and novelist with a background in film, theater, psychology, and marketing. He has a lifetime of experience in sleight of hand with cards and was a student of master magician Slydini. He studies cartomancy with Camelia Elias.

The Hypnotist

Simone Grace Seol

Good tarot readers are hypnotists.

Throw away the little white book.

The quality of a reading is proportional to your fear-lessness.

Forget about 'meanings' so you can go straight to ob-serving what strikes you.

Locate the point of tension, and the points of relief.

Observe what elements of the card repeat, mirror, con-nect, and contradict.

Let common sense tell you how the visual elements relate back to the question.

Talk less so that the other person can hear their own unconscious mind.

Don't step on someone else's trance. When you see fire between a card and someone else's eyes, get out of the way.

When the other person sighs with recognition, you say, "that's right."

Information gets forgotten; it's the feelings and dreams stirred up by the images that stay.

Support emotional responses with concrete evidence you see in the shapes.

If you're reading for someone else, never miss a change in their breath, or the fluttering of their eyelids.

If you're reading for yourself, never miss a change in your own breath, a fluttering of your eyelids.

A reading is not over until there is a silence that lands like a bird on St. Francis' shoulder.

When the cards smack you across the head, say thank you.

When a card insists on being a talisman, say yes and bow.

The tarot works via the placebo effect. Know what you suggest, and notice how the suggestion 'goes in.'

The tarot works beyond your table because of the placebo effect.

Kill your teacher. Read as only you can.

The only reason to read the cards is to live a more beautiful life.

> The Buddhist scholar Wonhyo says: The Ace of Cups is no different from a rotting skull.

*

SIMONE GRACE SEOL descends from a line of eminent Korean Buddhists (including Wonhyo), and less eminent shamans. California-born and New York-reared, she currently lives in Seoul as a tarot-hypnotist, writer and artist.

Ace of Cups by Simone Grace Seol

A Manifesto in Voices

Bent Sørensen

The first cut is the deepest.

Don't cut the deck twice.

Jack Kerouac said: "Try not get drunk outside yr own house." He was talking to himself, but it works for fortunetellers too.

Kerouac also said: "I always meet my Bodhisattvas in the street." Most of them are online now.

Van Morrison says: "There's only here, there's only now." Fortune-telling is not about the future, but about the present.

When the cards fall on the table, get out of the way.

Musashi said: "Think lightly of yourself and deeply of the world." Kerouac read Musashi, but he didn't take his advice. The fortune-teller should.

Musashi also said: "Do not pursue the taste of good food." He wasn't thinking straight. You can't think straight on an empty stomach.

Man does not live by cards alone.

Jesus said: "It is finished". He didn't consult the cards first.

When you have put your three cards down, it *is* finished.

Freud's client said: "It's not my Mother." It's always your Mother.

Don't read the cards for your Mother, unless she is dead.

The sitter says: "Does he love me?" The fortune-teller knows the answer before the cards fall.

The sitter says: "Will he be back?" The fortune-teller sharpens her sword.

The sitter says: "Does he still think of me?" The fortune-teller says: "Is he here with you now?"

You can ask the cards anything. The cards will answer, "Anything."

Derrida said: "I've not read many books, but the ones I've read, I read really well." The cards only speak one language, but they speak it really well.

The Surrealist Manifesto says: "Man proposes and dis-poses." The cards oppose and disclose.

You don't have to be mad to read the cards, but it sure helps.

I married the fortune-teller. My fortunes are told for free.

Frigg the Familiar says: "Mummy-Unit is the fortune-teller isn't she? And you're No. 2..."

*

BENT SØRENSEN regularly has conversations with his dog, old songs, and dead people like Freud and Jesus. He likes to quote them all.

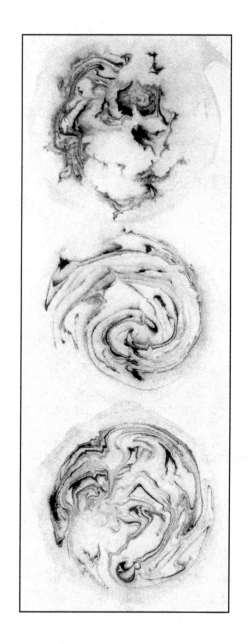

Three of Coins by Camelia Elias

Ishtar's Trick

Rachel Pollack

See what there is to see.

Hear what there is to hear.

Touch whatever you touch.

Speak the thing you must speak.

Speak only the thing you must speak.

The client knows what they want. Do not change their questions.

Keep moving.

The Tarot may be scary, but the Tarot is your friend. Or to put it another way, "Fear not! Ishtar is here."

Don't be afraid to tell the truth. Someone's life may depend on it.

What's true today may not be true tomorrow.

You can't go forward if you won't look back.

Keep your feet in tradition, and your head in the light.

The one forbidden rule of divination – do not predict the day and manner of a person's death.

The Tarot is a map of the Land of the Dead.

Be tricky.

Dazzle.

The Tarot will heal if you allow it.

From the back of the head, the Presence is below. Thus, the Presence is above, and glory fills the Earth. (from *Ha-Sefer Raziel Ha-Malakh, The Book of the Angel Raziel*)

Open your heart to the Sun.

Wake up!

It is always possible, at any moment, to see everything at once. Just don't count on it, or try to force it.

The eye can't hit what the hand can't see. Dream like a butterfly, go home like a bee.

*

RACHEL POLLACK is the author of 41 books, including two award-winning novels. She has also written a series of books about Tarot, a book of poetry, *Fortune's Lover*, and has translated, with scholar David Vine, Sophocles's *Oidipous Tyrannos*, under the title *Tyrant Oidipous* (also from EyeCorner Press). She has designed and drawn her own Tarot deck, *The Shining Tribe Tarot*, and with artist Robert Place she has created two more decks. She has taught and lectured on four continents. For eleven years she taught in Goddard College's MFA writing program. Rachel lives in New York's Hudson Valley.

Clarity

Cindie Chavez

A single card can speak volumes. Listen.

Also, you must hear your client. Listen deeply.

We're all fortune-tellers. Your client has been telling their own fortune forever. Recognize your client's ability to create.

Kings and Queens and time-machines, these magical cards. Be present in this moment.

You only think you're the one shuffling. Be aware that you are only a part of the process.

You can read a bowl of fruit if that suits you better – it's all just apples and oranges. Oracles are everywhere. Don't be too serious.

A deck in the hands is the beginning of magic. You are a conduit, be open.

There is an art to asking good questions and this makes all the difference. Learn to ask sharp questions.

Muddy questions bring confusing answers, and some-times smartass replies. Be clear.

If you ask the same question again and again you might be taken on a wild goose chase! Ask once.

Learn to say yes to yourself and to the cards. Look for the YES.

If you aren't certain of yourself you will never be cer-tain of the cards. Choose to be certain.

If you don't have confidence in yourself your client will not have confidence in you either. Choose to read with conviction.

Your relationship with cards will grow and strengthen in time. Relationships of all kinds take time and nurturing. Be willing to invest your time in this relationship.

Non-resistance is imperative to magic. BREATHE.

There are no "good cards" or "bad cards". There are just cards. Relax.

Light creates shadow. Don't be afraid of the dark.

You read the cards and the cards read you. Recognize when your own energy is affecting the message you are delivering. Be aware of the interplay of energies.

There are no mistakes. Stop worrying about whether you are "getting it right."

The cards bring enough mystery to the process. Speak plainly.

A simple message that seems basic and obvious may be revealing a big secret. Let it be easy.

> Juno's Peacock has feathers with hundreds of eyes. This reminds us that there are hundreds of ways to see every card. Have confidence in the way your two eyes see them.

*

CINDIE CHAVEZ reads cards, books, people, and whatever else strikes her fancy. When she isn't reading she enjoys making art, coaching people, creating sigils, trying to figure out her astrology chart, knitting, and writing essays and books.

The Peacock Sigil by Cindie Chavez

Killing the Fortune-Teller:
Rules, reversals and talking trees

Yi-Sung Oliver Ho

For every observation, find its opposite. Swords attack. Swords defend.

Draw attention to imbalance. You are the absence of emptiness.

Live as a student. No master exists.

Read for others more often than for teachers. Fluency develops through everyday conversation.

A deck consists of arbitrary, randomized images you turn into metaphors. At any time, anything can be something else.

Your interpretive system imposes order and rationality. Right now, everything is something else.

Convey confidence, knowledge and empathy. Lead the experience, and never cause harm.

When you think you know what you're doing, think: You don't. Never compete.

Communicate with concrete language and provide direct answers. State what the cards suggest.

Create metaphors for the other person to unpack. An answer exists only for the person asking the question.

Apply structures from other disciplines. Divine like a beekeeper, architect, astronaut.

Be formless. The cards, the question, and the other person structure the reading.

Vary your tempo, tactics and target to evade predictability. Anticipate and intercept cliché.

Strive for consistency and fulfill expectations. Allow the other person to see a familiar reflection.

Read only what exists as ink on paper. Cards depict still images.

Study widely to increase the radius of your interpretations. Movement happens in the space between cards.

Clarify your beliefs about divination. *What do you think you're doing?*

The only belief that matters belongs to the other person. What do *they* think you're doing?

Avoid bullshit. Seek to read rather than impress.

Risk it. Read without thought, make mistakes, and then ask why.

It isn't about you.

> Scientific evidence suggests trees communicate to one another through fungal and pheremonal networks. They send warnings, request help, and change behaviours in response. If a tree falls, the forest knows why.

*

YI-SUNG OLIVER HO has published more than a dozen books, including fiction, non-fiction and poetry. Currently, he works as a writer and editor at the Centre for Addiction and Mental Health in Canada.

~~Rules of~~ Engagement/ Disengagement/Engagement

Caitriona Reed

Lay down the cards – the game is up!

Let the cards speak among themselves.

Forget everything – open the floodgates of memory – let the flow carry you.

First thought – best thought!

Ask your sitter what they notice.

Everything is alive, everything is conscious, everything is connected, everything matters.

Look through the eyes you see in the cards.

In physics, time is an anomaly, its existence depends on gravity.

Lay down the cards – step outside of time – defy gravity.

There's a world inside the world you see – and inside that there's another – and another.

Things are what they seem – and then some.

Lay down the cards in the pause between your out-breath and in-breath.

Breathe in – follow what your body is saying.

Breath out – trust your own silence.

The cards speak the dialect of a universal language.

Sometimes it pretends to be untranslatable.

Lay down the cards – conflict is based on prior agree-ments.

Lay down the cards – heal the dead.

Lay down the cards – break your old loyalties.

Lay down the cards – the universe writes a love letter to itself.

The easier it is, the easier it is.

The path: Take any path and follow it until every path becomes your own, until all things are yours – all living belovèd until all paths take you along the path which is yourself.

*

CAITRÌONA REED is a Zen Teacher in the lineage of Thich Nhat Hanh. She has led trainings, workshops, and retreats worldwide. She mentors business owners, artists, and creative entrepreneurs who understand that success, creativity, and wellbeing, are an 'inside job'. As a 'woman of transgendered experience' she is fascinated by intersections and permeable boundaries. She is currently exploring the ground between plant medicine, tarot, and trance.

La Lune by Michele Benzamin-Miki

Cartomantic Harmonics

Sterling Clavelle

Allow surprises by adopting a sense of adventure. Wilfully seek out and manifest the "WTF?!?" The unexpected turn is always much more interesting.

Be inventive and ready to adapt: Say, for example, play additional cards or perhaps fewer than planned, or place them in different locations on the table, as the nature of the query and the associated drama evolves. Encourage harmonic feedback.

Document everything. Journal, photograph, record – especially your fortune-telling cards.

Non-preciousness with experimentation is paramount, regardless the hymn-book one abides to. Generate new ideas and theories, evaluate, throw them away and repeat, but don't forget to develop your good stuff.

Be certain, then declare. Or be brave enough to commit to well thought out mistakes. To fuck with hindsight.

Mostly disregard what the Little White Book says.

Mix and match your 'mancies, or try different decks together, or try using multiple same-decks in one shuffle.

Don't dilly dally. Deal and decode, diligently deliver directly without undue delay.

You can't un-see a card. It is ill advised to play, and then unplay a card – or peek at what might have turned up next. If you saw it, it happened. Deal with it. If it fucks with your narrative, tough shit: You will have to square it.

Always travel with a means of divination, be ever ready to improvise if you are caught at large without.

Recreate card layouts from dreams, even – and especially – if you have to fabricate the deck with which so to do.

Fortune-telling and reflective introspection are not mutually exclusive; they should both be practiced with vigour, in tandem – with a co-parasitic regard.

Abide no precept.

Read. Research. Turn cards. Ruminate. Repeat.

If the cards are the cogs, talcum powder is the grease. Apply as needed for superior glide. I can recommend Pinaud Clubman Talc for its classic barbershop attitude and dandyish floral notes. It also masks some stains and eases stale cigarette odour from those late nights in the back garden with friends.

Subvert, derail, uphold, prevail.

Be curious about visual grammar. Perhaps be fastidious, set your cards in tidy rows with even spaces between. Use a nice surface. Be unfurled and wild-ish when it is a choice you have made for your own appropriate and damned good reasons. Explain those reasons to no one.

Be confident with yourself and your skill. Humility is fine – but only ever in modest quantity.

Share what you discover. Be sure to credit yourself when you inspire others. Sure, keep some craftiness in tight proximity, but not all. Let the Right Ones In.

Playfulness and irreverence are amongst the strongest expressions cards allow us. A canny pun extracted from a few cards can be as insightful and convincing as any well-crafted body of documented evidence.

Perhaps consider the non-dualistic characteristics of a vegan diet. Thinking your own dietary ideas through and being true to yourself at all times may be more useful.

Cultivate phlegmatic vacuity, so to encourage the contiguous space between and around the cards. Observe.

*

STERLING CLAVELLE is a student of Aradia Academy and resident of Lethbridge Alberta, deep in Canada's conservative Bible Belt. He is much prouder of his birthplace, Winnipeg Manitoba – a veritable hotbed of pinkos, punk rockers, and socialism.

Code of the Desert

Debi Ann Scott

POISONOUS CREATURES: Don't balk at any question, be cunning.

WASHES: Empty mind and an open heart.

WILDFIRES: Be fearless. Confidence begets answers.

MIRAGE: Be clear. Don't read what is not there.

TRAILS: Stick with a method, then find your own style.

WILDERNESS: Do not wander without purpose.

DRY HEAT: Feel it – Be it – See it.

COPPER: Be the conductor.

SUN: An authority is not the place to find the answers.

Cactus: Be sharp and precise.

Flash flood: Eliminate expectations and distractions.

Scout: Scan and find the peculiar.

Adobe: Build a solid foundation.

Dust Devil: Break the rules.

Borderlands: Navigate borders to and fro.

Rainbow: Follow the colors.

Flatlands: When lost, look through a Hag Stone.

Vista: Ideology is not your ally.

Petroglyphs: Don't dazzle with history and symbols. Find confirmation.

Mountains: Make yourself available for the mysterious.

Indigenous people: Be a storyteller, don't tell stories.

> **The Scorpion** says: Know your nature or you will get stung.

*

DEBI ANN SCOTT is a seeker, experiencer, fortuneteller and sitter with the mystery. She lives in the Southwest USA Arizona, communing with the saguaros and energies of the desert. She's retired, and her journey is herself. The image of the scorpio here is her own art.

Cards Say, "You Belong"

James Wells

A deck of cards is not a belief system or creed, it is simply a tool.

All cards are neutral. One's questions make them lean toward "negative" or "positive".

Neither the cards nor "fate" make things happen; people cause life to happen.

A card's concept or interpretation can be more than a noun; it can be verb or process.

A card's concept or interpretation can be more than a statement; it can ask us questions.

Study more than cards: myths, poetry, psychology, nature, mathematics, astrology, your life...

You are simply a guide; the querent is the real expert on her or his life.

The cards illuminate life's options; awareness of more choices equals more power.

It starts with a yearning, a deep ache to change or maintain something in one's life.

Curiosity blossoms – yearning morphs into questions – open mind and heart.

Underlying these are, "What's real? Who am I? Why am I here? What is my role?"

Maximum structure – agreed-upon intention, layout, and time frame – for maximum flow.

Clear context is your friend; the cards alone are not enough. It comes back to this.

Intensification of awareness, of consciousness, is the card reading's main aim.

Show up and be present; choose to be with the cards, questions, client, Life's whispers.

Open yourself to the path of heart and compassion, to the way of deepest meaning.

Notice and express what is true without placing blame or casting judgement.

Though you set a clear intention, be open to the surprise outcome that flows in.

Card encounters help shape meaning, define a system we can apply to real life.

Living this personal system can assist the process of personal evolution.

One's personal evolution enhances our collective evolution.

As each card is vital to the deck, each person is a vital component of the cosmos.

*

JAMES WELLS is an evolutionary tarot consultant and circle process practitioner in Toronto. Dedicated to guiding individuals and groups to remember their innate wisdom, creativity, and wholeness, he is the author of *Tarot for Manifestation* and *Tarot Circle Encounters* and a contributor to various anthologies. In his "me time", he enjoys trees, good food, reading, writing, and leisurely walks.

Aphorisms of the Oracle

Natalia Forty

The art of divining starts with vision.

The sharpness of your vision determines what you see.

Next to vision come the ears. How you listen to the question defines the oracle.

Without a question there is no oracle.

The qualities for divining are sight and hearing. Afterward, come the cards.

It is a true saying that the cards are only as useful as the diviner.

It is even truer to confess that a good diviner will divine with anything.

The art lies in how the diviner situates the sight, what is seen, with the question.

The oracle knows. Divining rests in the power of now, within the moment the question is articulated.

Of the cards, they contain infinite possibilities but only in as much as the diviner unlocks them.

With the cards come images, with images words. Pairing words with images is the key that unlocks the message.

A tarot reading is the entangling of image and word, what is seen with what is spoken.

Like the cards, words are only as useful as a person is at orchestrating them.

In a reading, the words must answer the question FIRST.

The question is answered by looking at the images, and arriving at what in the images expresses the answer to the question.

When the words start meeting your vision, your role as a diviner is to cull the superfluous, keeping only the essential.

The words you enunciate must speak of what arrives at the heart of the matter.

The oracle's place lies at the heart of the matter.

Lastly comes the voice. Communicating the words to the question should be given the same care as listening to the question.

Divination is the art of sight, hearing, images, words, articulation, *in medias res.*

In essence, I reiterate, the diviner can arrive at the oracle with anything, be it rosemary sticks, bones, leaves, dice, charms, birds.

> The jaguar says: "Learn to listen, see, and move like an elegant hunter in the twilight of the rainforest that waits for the precise moment to pounce and sieze the meal."

*

NATALIA FORTY is a writer, reader, and divinatrix, born in a small island in the Caribbean, surrounded by the lull of waves and the curved grace of palm trees. She has an MA in Literary Theory and Criticism near completion. She strives to live with a sense of mystery and wonder, while firmly grasping a book.

The Smell of Form

Ryan Edward

Cards are products of design, governed by divine design.
Interpret by way of design.

Line carries the narrative. Follow the flow.

Direction sets motion. Ride along.

Form follows function. Have purpose.

Proportion imposes hierarchy. Weigh what's important.

Proximity relates. Measure the distance.

Texture adds interest. Get gritty.

Color paints tone. Feel the mood.

Balance provides an equilibrium. Locate the fulcrum.

Space breathes. Exhale.

Pattern repeats with consistency. Predict what's certain.

Rhythm repeats with variety. Find the beat.

Unity solidifies. Check the foundation.

Emphasis commands attention. Highlight the obvious.

Contrast sharpens. Compare what's different.

Alignment levels. Solve for the common denominator.

Innovation inspires. Be fresh.

Approachability is understable. Relate.

Honesty speaks truth. Don't hold back.

Details matter. Specify.

Minimalism simplifies. Read as little as possible.

Jasmine says: The sweet smell of death blends with everything.

*

RYAN EDWARD is an always curious designer from St. Louis who plays in the crossroads of art, design, fortune telling, cards, and botanicals. One part novice to three parts earnest nerd, he makes cards, grows herbs, and blends fragrance for his shop, Inset. His image here.

The Emancipated Eye

Sherryl Smith

Know each card's heart like you know your lover's heart. Look into the card deeply; with reverence.

Every card has its core energy – respect it! The 3 of Cups is not interchangeable with the 10 of Swords. Cards don't mean just anything depending on your whims.

Two cards – one for each eye. Turn the cards over simultaneously so they hit your retina together.

Read the patterns – not the cards. Like the flight of birds or the throw of bones, the lines, shapes, colors and gestures of the cards reflect the moment's pattern.

Read the space between the cards. Feel the yearning, the repulsion, the clash – the tension of the force field.

Kick a hole in the wall of your perceptions. Let fresh air rush in along with dragonflies, pollen and spider silk. Whatever enters, let it speak with its own voice.

First thought – best thought. Grasp the first thought or image that flits through your mind. Then...

Blurt it out. Say what you see with no filters.

Every card has its dance. Set the cards in motion so they spin, shimmer, writhe, vibrate.

Reading is an all-body experience. Notice your gut twisting, hairs standing on end, skin prickling.

Exquisite attention. Let your eyes roam lovingly over the card, soaking in every detail.

Zen looking. Be open to it all. Don't latch on to the first obvious thing.

Beginner's mind. With each reading you parachute into a new reality.

Get out of the story. Let the cards reframe the context.

Get out of the way. Be the channel, not the interpreter.

Spreads entangle you in linear time. By the time you read the last card you're a different person from the one who laid the cards down. So...

Pick and read cards one at a time. Surf the changing energy.

Each card unlocks a labyrinth of questions. Better a dialog than oracular pronouncements.

It's just the damn image! It's not the book meanings, or the esoteric correspondences, or the personal associations.

Images are a diving bell to the deepest layers of the psyche. Your fate lies in your pre-verbal, cellular memories that only an image can access.

The cards are an externalized dream, spread on the table, offering themselves up for close examination.

Kandinsky says: "If the inadequately developed eye cannot experience deeply, it will not be able to emancipate itself from the material plane in order to perceive the indefinable space."

Ace of Hearts by Merete Veian

*

SHERRYL SMITH began an intense, 45-year affair with tarot after encountering the Aquarian deck on a California beach. Three decades later the relationship transformed dramatically when she discovered tarot's 600-year history. Sherryl shares the results of her research, and teaches techniques for reading with historic decks at her blog, *Tarot Heritage.*

The Thermodynamics of Card Divination

Geoff Krueger

ABSTRACT

Certain skills are required to find the brittle whispers in the in-between permeating beneath the stars.

INTRODUCTION

Entropy is generally defined as 'waste heat' or friction/resistance, inhibiting flow and is a measure of unintended consequences and impermanence.

The physical law of the Conservation of Energy applies to divination, as all readings generate entropy.

A reading is a manifested omen, being a reflection of energy, frequency and vibration.

The entropy of a reading rises in proportion to the active timeline and the perceived duality.

The more one identifies, or attaches, to a card image, the greater the entropy.

METHODS

A reading can be expressed as an equation:

QUESTION = CARD SPREAD

Hence, the quality of the interpretation is equal to the quality of the question.

An intentional breath, a pulse, is the foundation of agency.

The exercise of agency is considered "An impossible thing."

Modifying or creating new lines of gravity is the result of agency.

Effortless (practiced) alignment with lines of gravity is a ritual.

Who is doing what to whom is also a question of habit vs. agency.

The best questions generate high acceptance and low entropy.

Excessive focus increases expectation, while acceptance fosters discernment.

A question posed to a spread is akin to a sonar net cast into the ocean. The reading seeks the question as much as the querent seeks an answer.

RESULTS

Reading outcomes do not express duality. Duality only exists as a measurement of the querent's resistance to flow.

Attachments generate friction, manifesting as resistance and entropy.

As flowing water follows lines of gravity, one only needs to look to the water to find flow.

DISCUSSION

There is always water flowing under the ice. Entropy thins this ice, creating sudden change from seemingly insignificant inputs.

Ultimately the card images represent nothing tangible. It is the interaction of the images with each other that determines the narrative, in conjunction with the question.

There is constant flux. A reading expands the extended present to allow the determination of speed and direction in a condition of stillness.

The Fox does not chase a desired outcome. She asks how to adjust the environment to make the outcome inevitable.

*

GEOFF KRUEGER was born in 1970. He studied Molecular Biology at the University of Maryland and Biotechnology at the Johns Hopkins University. He currently works as a Laboratory Systems Analyst and practices biodynamic permaculture on his urban farm in Milwaukie, Oregon. Most of his inspiration springs from his daily bicycle rides along the Willamette River.

Leave the Textbooks Behind
Beverly Frable

The Fool – **EXPLORE** – How does the meaning of the images change when you start anew, reading what you see, not what you learned?

The Magician – **SHAPE** – Are there shapes presented and shared between the images that add significance in previously unseen ways?

The High Priestess – **SUBTLETY** – What appears in the background? Of what significance are those images that are less overt, not as prominently displayed?

The Empress – **SOFT** – Do the images present a sense of warmth, nurturing, protection, compassion, or supportive? Or....

The Emperor – **HARD** – Do the images portray a sense of being firm, distant, competitive, or impacting?

The Hierophant – **ROLE** – Do the images convey one of offering input or seeking insight? An "answer to" or a "question about?"

The Lovers – **OPTION** – Are the images flowing together or do they show a conflict, perhaps as though a choice or decision point is immanent?

The Chariot – **SPEED** – Is there a sense of moving fast (greater number of Batons/Swords) or more towards being slow (mostly Cups/Coins)?

Justice – **VALUES** – What's happening pertaining to the numerical values of the cards? Are there dramatic jumps up/down?

The Hermit – **DIRECTION** – How does the direction portrayed by the images impact the significance?

The Wheel of Fortune – **ORDER** – What images proceed or follow the central images and might that impact the interpretation?

Strength – **POWER** – What is the sense of strength or softness? Are you seeing displays of power or more oriented toward meekness?

The Hanged Man – **PERCEPTION** – Does being still, taking a moment and focusing on the image somehow alter how it appears or presents itself?

Death – **ENDURANCE** – Are the images portraying a sense of vitality, acceptance, resolution or more of a resignation, submission, surrender?

Temperance – **FLOW** – How might the flow of colors or even the lack of colors flowing influence the message?

The Devil – **RELATIONSHIP** – Do the images give a sense of authority, dominance, control or one of cooperation, collaboration?

The Tower – **STABILITY** – Is there a perception of chaos, discord, confusion, turmoil or do the images demonstrate a peace, calmness, harmony?

The Star – **INSPIRATION** – Do the images spark a sense of healing, encouragement, gratitude or more of a tone of thanklessness, hopelessness?

The Moon – **SHADING** – How is the shading used to express the intention of the image? Are there shadows? Or perhaps a lack of shading?

The Sun – CONTRAST – What colors do the images have in common? Are they mostly bright? What tone is set through the choice of the colors?

Judgment – AWARENESS – What level of comprehension is suggested through the images? One of seeking? Contemplation? Or a more confident awareness such as comprehension.

The World – NATURE – What forms of nature are represented in the images? What nature is shared between the images? Which are unique?

THE MOST IMPORTANT RULE: Trust Yourself.

*

BEVERLY FRABLE is a professional tarot consultant, having studied divination while attending tarot events throughout the US and also under the direction of many of the world's renowned authorities on cartomancy. She is currently focussed on preparing learning opportunities for others on subjects as varied as introductions to, comparisons, and combination readings between Tarot, Lenormand, Kipper and Playing Cards – and the cultural impacts/influences of each including a brief history of divination.

Twenty-One Possible Steps to Mirth

Adam Wolkoff

Buy a random tarot deck.

Unsuccessfully attempt to unlock its secrets using the included, incomprehensible Little White Book. Lose the deck in a drawer and walk away.

Years later, buy another deck. Throw away the Little White Book with a laugh. Riffle the cards face up through your hands, considering the pictures and the possibilities.

Believe that tarot is a "system" and that every card has discrete "meaning" as expressed through defined "spreads."

Purchase tarot books by people you've never met to teach you said system, meaning and spreads. Try to memorize the contents.

Fail the attempt.

Give up on tarot books.

Give up on discrete meanings and defined spreads.

Lie on your back in bed, after the alarm clock has rung and the snooze button smashed. Bring your right foot up and place it next to your left knee. Realize that you have become The Hanged Man.

See your world reflected in every card.

Encounter every card reflected in your world.

Nod with recognition when you see each other.

Shuffle your deck, ask a question, then lay three cards face down on the table.

Look sharp: There's no such thing as coincidence. "Know what is in front of your face and what is hidden from you will be disclosed." – Gospel of Thomas, 5

Read your cards to answer your question. Eureka! You're a card reader!

Begin to read for others. Resist the temptation to repeat Steps 4-7.

If reading in exchange for money, adopt a "pay first/ no refunds" policy.

Every querent has a question – no question, no reading.

Every question has an answer – it's the one in the cards right in front of you.

When the question is answered, the reading is done.

When the reading is done, stop talking.

The Devil says: The truth hurts, but it's still the truth.

*

ADAM WOLKOFF is a magician, father, judge, husband, photographer, cook, son, card-slinger and cat-herder (though not necessarily in that order). He plans to spend his next fifty years unlearning everything he learned in his first fifty years.

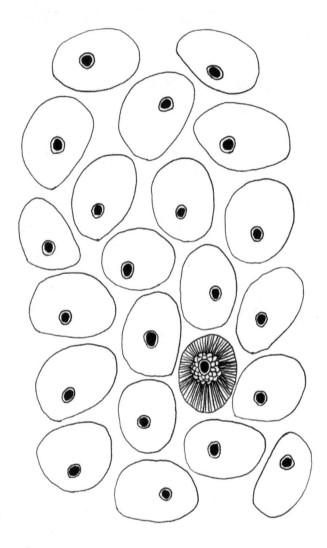

21 + 1 by Merete Veian

Make it Beautiful

Fortuna Sawahata

Draw

First, fear no cards. Fear not to read. Send the ego on a playdate. Get shuffling. You have no idea. Really.

Listen. What was the question? Is there a question under the question?

Draw. Look at what's on the table, magically and practically – through image, find the syntax of the reading.

Think. Where does the meaning come from in this reading? From the function of the card, or from the form? From the colour, the number, the image?

Notice. ('Read the damn cards.')

SELECT. Where does your eye take you? What 'feels' significant in this reading?

CUT

Cut as much of your attachment to 'giving a good reading' as you can. Especially if it's for yourself.

DISCERN. What's the story here? Where are the relationships? Is your intuition, your Guidance, shouting or pointing at anything? Does your Mind agree?

ASK. The above eight pointers have occurred within the first minute of a reading. You're the captain of this ship. Get the one you are reading for – including yourself – to answer any clarifying questions.

WEIGH. Balance the chunks of information accessed by your questions, with what your eyes see and your Mind knows.

FORMULATE. The sentence, the mantra, the swift cut that lops off all the nonsense and reveals the issue, uncorseted by niceness or other concerns.

DELIVER. The sharpest, shortest sentence you can.

STUN. Yourself and the client. Because indeed, 'how *could* you know [fill in blank]'.

Short-cut. Back to the original question. Has it been answered?

Know. What is the kindest cut of all? The one that liberates us and our client from illusion. Most of us will go a far piece to avoid that cut. So...

Sheathe

Remember. After-care is a part of your reading. You wouldn't amputate someone's illusion without proper cauterization, right?

Massage. Apply your most suave words to the harder truth you may just have delivered.

Offer. To look deeper at whatever angle or corner of the reading has dug up (or cut up) a significant piece of information, possibility, or emotion for the client.

Share. Is there a practice, book, herb, sexual position, form of exercise or alcohol that you have used and think might be useful to the client?

Assign. 'Try this. See how it works for you over the next 8 weeks.' (Practically, it's a good way to build relationships with folks who might want repeat consultations.)

GET OUTTA THERE. Send photos/recordings of the session on as the final 'stroke' of the reading.

The Water says 'One part of me is all parts of me. Deep and shallow, cold and warm, frozen and flowing – dive into paradox and figure out if you have to swim, bathe, or skate during this reading.'

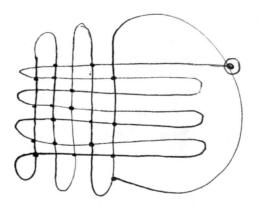

*

FORTUNA SAWAHATA is a witch, a writer, a cartomancer, an artist, and a perpetual student. She learns by teaching: private students of Anderson Feri Tradition, public groups at Reclaiming witchcamps and workshops. She learns by learning – with Camelia Elias, of course – and ongoing efforts with human and otherworldly teachers. Cranky, introverted, green-eyed Japanese-American born in L.A., living in Rotterdam in the Netherlands. Stellium in Libra in the first house. Fire Rooster. Her own sigil here.

Uncorking 'Nothing'

Devon Patel

Have a question? Be sure you want the answer in the first place.

Leave all sense of dominance, submission, right or wrong, black or white, any polarity in the waiting room. You are here for answers not a debate. All of your 'belongings' will be waiting for you when you come back.

Forget who you are. Certifications, identity, gender, sexuality, emotion, culture, fears, insecurities, etc. None of it is the question. None of it is relevant when you receive your answer.

Stretch. Prepare your body to manipulate. Having a good sense of mobility before approaching the cards. Shake it all off.

Meditate. Be still. Be silent. Be uninvolved. Be naked. The space has been set and you're unattached. You're a vessel, a message in a bottle, yet instead of a letter, you hold one question and only that question. Your body is the glass bottle. Everything around you slides off your body. The question remains dry and unharmed within you.

Shuffle the cards. You're nothing, and you're ready to read the damn cards.

Pop the cork off and reveal your question and only the question.

Look at the cards. Unattached from the world (or worlds) around you, what do you see? Don't fight it, just use your senses.

Do these sensations empower or disempower you? Are you drooling to get a word out? If so, put the cards back in their case and go back to step 1.

You are nothing. How does nothing go from point A to point B? It just does, as it is not involved or attached to any fears, obstacles, passions, or sense of confidence. Nothing is attached to nothing.

If 'nothing' can do anything and come from anything or anywhere, then what is your question in relation to what the cards say? Was your question even worth asking? Does it even matter? Are you saying nothing despite having this question?

You're nothing, but nothing continues to be nothing unless action is set in place.

Still want answers and movement? Great, in relation to the question, what do the cards show by way of actions you can perform?

Are these actions reminiscent of actions you perform at work? At home? With your lover? With your family? With your friends? Do they bring back memories? Are they more than the action itself? Go back to step 1.

Like you, these actions are nothing and hold no symbolic influences or meaning. They are physical movements of doing. Just do the damn task in relation to "this is what I want" and "this is how you get that very damn thing".

Breathe. There, you did it. You showed yourself how to do something in relation to your intention. After all, that was what you wanted, right? That breathing isn't done in comparison to who you envy. It isn't done to show off. It isn't done to hide your fears and insecurities. It's done to supply your body with oxygen and that's that. You did that on your own. You don't need to think about it.

Look at the cards once again with the question and only the question in mind. Breathe, and put the cards away.

Meditate... again. Be still. Be silent. Be uninvolved. Be naked. You now know what you want, you now know what to do.

Go back to the waiting room where you left your 'be-longings'. I told you they'd be waiting for you when you were done. Feel free to throw out anything that might be redundant, unrelated, too heavy, for your trip back.

Pack lightly when embarking on another journey.

Nothing says: It can be something. That something is up to YOU to decide.

*

DEVON PATEL is not in the the business of public fortune-telling, but he is a man who finds himself wound up in a world full of cultural influences, reading cards. He is familiar with the teachings of Aradia Academy, and he draws as well on discourses ranging from mindfulness philosophy to Dialectical Behavior Therapy.

Moon Reading

Archie Leung

The goal of reading cards and the Moon is to have fun.

The cards and the Moon show, because they hide.

People read the Moon for a sense of temporal progression. People read the cards for a fragment of eternity.

The Moon reflects, so do the cards.

You hang on to the moonlight when you walk in the dark. You hold on to the cards when you walk in the dark.

Always use what you see. Don't think it's the Man in the Moon because others say so.

Point to the Moon and you will have your ear cut. Go to the cards and you will, well, be cut, but in a good way.

Rise as high as the Moon so you can see what's on the table.

What seems to be missing in a spread gives a wealth of information, like the New Moon.

You can keep your fantasies until you can see the far side of the Moon. You can keep your fantasies until you turn over the cards.

Pray to the Moon to make you as cold as she is, so you will be useful.

The Moon can be the Ace of Coins. After all, one needs to take a break after some dog has barked at you for eternity.

The cards show as little light in your future as an eclipse? No worries, the Moon will change her face one day.

The Moon is silent and serene, because you don't have a question.

If the Moon baffles you with her everlasting smile, look at her hard, and then go back to your question. She will have had enough of it and tell you the answer.

Practise reading the cards as often as the Moon rises.

The Moon is clear, brilliant, and beautiful, but no one said she is nice.

Is it the Moon, the looking glass, the computer screen, the footbath or the spotlight?

All of the above.

There is a Moon in the water because there's a Moon in the sky. There are meanings in the cards because there is a context.

"The Moon is the Moon." When in doubt, state the obvious, and go from there.

> The Hare in the Moon says, "without a context, how can you tell if I'm female or male?"

*

ARCHIE LEUNG was born in Hong Kong and learned how to read the Tarot at a young age. However, he decided he was no good for cartomancy until he stumbled across Aradia Academy. Now he is an avid card reader, especially playing cards.

Mystery Machine

Andrew McGregor

Tarot is a machine that runs on mystery and spits out truth!

It reveals itself only at co-ordinates in time and space with intention.

Others might call intention a question.

Great intentions clarify mystery.

Poor intentions multiply mystery.

Being wrong is okay if you know why it happened

Either way mystery always remains.

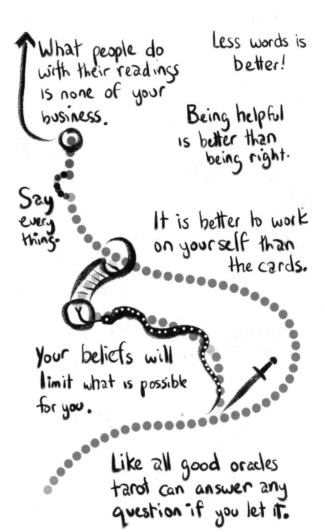

What people do with their readings is none of your business.

Less words is better!

Being helpful is better than being right.

Say everything.

It is better to work on yourself than the cards.

Your beliefs will limit what is possible for you.

Like all good oracles tarot can answer any question if you let it.

Boundaries are
everything

They keep you
accountable to
your intention.

They
keep
you
grounded

They sustain your
relationship to
the cards

They highlight
where you need
to work on
yourself.

They help you keep your faith.

They help you set better intentions

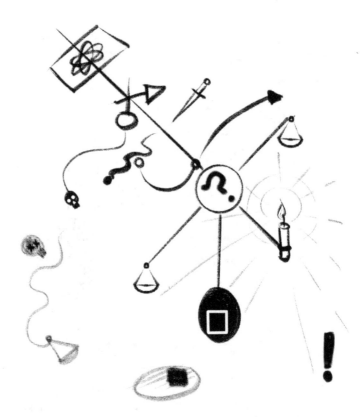

Andrew McGregor is a servant of the mysteries. He offers teaching and reading from his esoteric gift shop.

Dog's Wisdom

Jane Green

Robert Benchley says: "A dog teaches a boy three things, fidelity, perseverance, and to turn around three times before lying down." So too with fortune telling: Practice the first two daily, and turn around three cards.

Work like a surgeon. They concentrate on one thing and one thing only: their patient on the table. Concentrate only on your client and the cards which show up for them.

Focus your attention; otherwise you may miss something. When fortune-telling, it's OK to forget about your mother, dinner, etcetera – in fact it's essential to forget.

Work like a plumber. Charge for your work. But if you find a plumber who works for free, do let us all know.

Expect the unexpected. Even the client who, 5 minutes into her time, decided to breast-feed her baby for the rest of the session. Don't do the same.

Ritual or no ritual. It's up to you and it's perfectly possible to give a great reading in a railway station coffee shop. Grab your Jodo, and off you go.

Don't do anything new or 'not you' with a client. Practice and test first.

Dogs like trees for one reason – well, maybe more. You can't read on a full bladder.

Dogs love to nap. You can't read when you're tired.

Bertrand Russell says: "The good life is one inspired by love and guided by knowledge." Love your fortune-telling and don't stop studying. If you stop loving, take a break.

Give yourself time and stability. Ensure enough time for study and readings. When in life you meet instability, manage it or don't read. It's not fair on you or your client if you "fit them in" and rush the reading. They will know, and it isn't professional.

Read like a detective. Evidence every thing you say. Learn non-verbal communication and read the clues your client gives you.

Dogs stretch before getting going. Do the same, stretch and breathe before and between each client. Factor in time to do this.

Be aware of your own biases – the lens through which you view the world.

Be aware of what you know – or think you know about your clients.

Stop, Look and Listen is vital at a railway line crossing. Do the same. Stop. Look at the client and cards. Listen to the question. Listen deeply to the client.

Thomas Tusser says: "A fool and his money are soon parted." Choose your teachers, mentors, and studies wisely.

James Thurber says: "A dog has seldom been successful in pulling man up to its level of sagacity, but man has frequently dragged the dog down to his." Be like the dog, be sagacious in your readings, and choose similar traits in your teachers and colleagues.

Be ethical. Your clients are trusting you with their questions, and as a reader. Be aware of any legal requirements when reading. Set out your contract of confidentiality before you begin. Get insurance.

Develop your own style, and be happy with that. Be yourself and let your whole self show up. The magic is in you.

Be like the dog – after your reading, turn around three times, i.e. detach and remain free from attachment and outcomes.

> Dog's wisdom on life: "If, after all this, something goes wrong, kick some grass over it and carry on."

*

JANE GREEN has worked with divination, Reiki, NLP, dowsing, crystals and many types of fortune-telling with cards for nearly 30 years. She has learned from many masters, some of which were fortunate enough to be dogs.

Fortune-Telling in Strange Coffee Houses

Charles Webb

Get into character. The ego/persona is very much like a fictitious character in a play or movie. It can be re-written/directed/performed, etc. Create a "fortune-teller" persona for yourself. Method act.

Get into "costume." Nothing too outrageous... just distinctively different from everyday attire.

Pick a coffee house that you have never been in before, but looks ripe for customer tarot readings. Go in and order an espresso.

Look for a vacant table that would be good for readings, highly visible... by a window possibly.

Sit at the table and pull out your cards. Do not ask permission. If there is a problem, ask for forgiveness.

Pre-arrange for a friend to come in, order a coffee, then approach you, ask about the cards, and ask for a reading. Ask the person to sit and do a reading for them.

Notice if the other customers, staff, etc. are watching you.

Usually, the manager or owner will come to your table and ask what you are doing.

You explain that you are just having coffee and doing free readings if anyone wants them. This attracts more attention from the other customers. A few people stop at the window, look, then come in.

The owner/manager notices this and says OK. Offer to do a reading for the owner/manager. He/she declines.

The friend/customer you have been reading for leaves. You shuffle the cards and look around.

A shy customer approaches your table. You motion her over, then motion for her to sit down.

She sits and explains that she has never done this kind of thing before... is it dangerous?

You reassure her that a tarot reading is not dangerous (you lie a little), and what would she like to know... what is her question.

She presents you with a question.

You shuffle the deck and have her cut the cards, then lay down three cards in front of her.

She recoils a little and asks what they mean.

You read the cards and ask her if she has any questions.

She asks a few questions, which you answer.

She thanks you and leaves the table.

Another customer approaches... then another...

> At some point, you simply put you deck away, get up and leave the coffee house. You still have customers waiting for readings, wondering why you are leaving. You don't look back.

*

CHARLES WEBB operates a film, video and digital media production company in San Francisco. He has written, produced, directed and photographed projects in the US, Europe and China that encompass diverse genres. He also holds a masters degree in psychobiology and is the creator of the "reality handling" method known as Cinemorphics, which uses film and theater techniques to re-write, re-direct, re-produce, one's persona, ego, self.

Justice from The Trickster Marseille *by Charles Webb*

The Clear Question

Veronica Chamberlain

Ask the cards a clear and well-formulated question so that you will receive a clear answer.

Stick to a clear question.

Ask a question about the future, ask for advice, ask for magical intention, ask anything and the tarot will answer.

Just be clear with your question.

Use a 3-card spread. Use a 9-card spread. Use many cards in the spread...

Use a clear question for a precise answer.

Read the images on the cards and connect them together to formulate a clear answer derived from your
question.

So be clear with your question.

Find the evidence in the cards from your question that
will match your answer.

Be clear with the question.

Do not keep asking the same question to the cards
because you didn't like the answer.

A clear question will invite the clear answer that you
need.

Trust in the first answer you get from your question.

Trust in a clear question.

Do not judge a sitter's question, as it is the sitter's
reading.

Help the sitter to formulate a clear question.

Be fearless when consulting the tarot cards.

Ask clear and fearless questions.

As a reader detach from a tarot reading once it's done and move on to the next one.

Move on with clear questions for the tarot.

The one more rule for reading tarot is there are no set rules.

Yet still ask the tarot a clear question.

*

VERONICA CHAMBERLAIN is a diviner who likes to ask her tools and cards clear questions so that she can receive clear answers. She has studied under the mentorship of Camelia Elias for the last 5 years. She named her dog after Camelia and she calls her Cammy for short. How magical is that?

Sigil by Veronica Chamberlain

The Shape of the Loom

Markus Pfeil

Your words shape reality. Choose them sharply.

You reveal secrets. Disclose them truthfully.

You stir the cauldron. Observe what brews carefully.

You rule the reading. Be true and get out of the way.

You are being taught as well. Listen and accept the teaching.

You will be in doubt. Think of the question and use Occams razor. Keep it simple.

You will get in the flow. Let it carry you, but not away.

Your sense of right and wrong will be challenged. Stay out of the reading's way.

You will not know sometimes. You do not need to look elsewhere, it is all in the cards.

There will be the good and the bad. Do not hold any back.

You will be opposed. Stay true to the cards and your reading and do not oppose back.

You will get stuck. Remember the question and take the card literally.

Readings will be grim. They should be, and you see the way beyond.

People will know better. They do, and you are reading the cards.

You will run against convention. Do it and read like you don't care.

You will shatter dreams. Be compassionate and stay true.

The Cards are your stars to sail by. You are not the star.

You will know things from within. Heed them and check for their truth in the cards.

Your ego will interfere. Love it for its interference and send it away.

You will give counsel. Know in advance what you will counsel on and what not.

Everyone will come. Know the value of what you do and act accordingly.

Spider says: Read the cards like weaving a web. Do a careful job and what you catch will stick.

*

MARKUS PFEIL is 46 years old and lives in the south of Germany with his family. He is a physicist by education, currently teaching and researching in electrical engineering and informatics. He is also a Druid, a Musician and a Magician. Overall, he is a jack of many trades. And master of none.

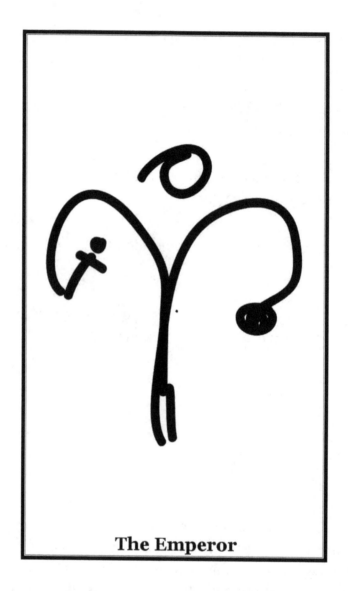

The Emperor

The Emperor by Markus Pfeil

The Arcana One by One

Shelley Ruelle

THE FOOL. Start. You can only read about reading for so long; put cards on the table.

THE MAGICIAN. You have all the tools you need. Stop searching for what's missing and use what you already have.

THE HIGH PRIESTESS. Be the gateway for the message. You're the conduit, not the source, so focus on the visually verifiable story in the images.

THE EMPRESS. Ground your readings in practical language. People want real-world answers.

THE EMPEROR. Own your authority as a reader. If you can't say what you see with confidence, practice more.

THE HIEROPHANT. Seek out a teacher. You can always learn something new.

THE LOVERS. When faced with a choice, pull another card. Clarity can come when 1+1=3.

THE CHARIOT. Get on the same page before charging forward. If two horses pull in opposite directions, you won't move.

STRENGTH. Explore the truths in polar opposites; they are one and the same. Strength is vulnerability.

THE HERMIT. Stop listening to everyone else and ask yourself. Great readers access their own center, where insight resides.

WHEEL OF FORTUNE. What goes up, must come down. There's no moral judgement of good and bad in tarot, only constant movement.

JUSTICE. Take the emotion out of it. Reading isn't about how you feel, it's about what you see.

THE HANGED MAN. When you don't know what to do, be still. Sometimes waiting is the most effective action.

DEATH. When there's no more to say, stop. Endings are there for a reason; don't prolong them.

TEMPERANCE. Extremes in one direction or another don't produce good readings. Find a balance between your intellect and your heart.

THE DEVIL. Suspend control and let the cards speak. Placing restrictions on or manipulating what emerges can defeat the purpose.

THE TOWER. Cards love to break things down; let them. Breaking down paves the way for building up.

THE STAR. Be aware of the role cards play in people's hopes. Sometimes your sitter just wants permission to do what he or she is going to do anyway, but that's not your business.

THE MOON. Embrace readings that leave you stumped and lost. Allow meaning to unfold, rather than demanding it adhere to your personal timeline.

THE SUN. Lighten up. This is not rocket science. Don't take yourself, or your cards, too seriously.

JUDGEMENT. If you're reading this, it's because you've been called to the cards. Keep hearing that call, and keep rising up from the dead to answer.

YGGDRASIL says: Ride the horse wherever it takes you. You're just the passenger, so take in the view before it's all over.

*

SHELLEY RUELLE has been reading cards since the year 2000, when she was gifted a Rider-Waite-Smith deck. In her work with the cards, she aims to provide people with practical insights so they can make empowered, conscious decisions. How the story always gets right to the heart of the matter is the magic.

Panoramic View

Dorian Broadway

Cartomancy is the examination of life and how it translates into language through cards.

Through acceptance of non-attachment you can see within the cards an accurate reflection of life.

Engage the cards to inquisitively explore this reflection.

The more specific your expression of inquisition, the more specific the translation of advice.

The art of reading is the art of conversation.

The conversation is best engaged without judgment.

Precision of sight, hearing, and voice are vital to this conversation.

Allow the cards to be as panes in a window.

Peer through the entire window, rather than through only one pane.

The cards reveal a panorama of insight.

The panorama expands through awareness of language.

A question is a pause for direction. A reading is a map. The cards are coordinates.

To throw down the cards is to send your spirit across the hedge into the Other realm.

To pack them up is to return to your body.

Be unafraid to say what you see.

Be unafraid to say nothing until you do see.

Read the cards without mercy, but with certainty of compassion.

Allow your intuition to serve as adjunct to your deductive reasoning.

Forsake alacrity in favor of composed discernment.

Define a crystal-clear method in which to read the cards.

Bend, break, and fuck this method whenever it controverts good judgment.

At the crossroads the black bitch howls. Speak and allow the cards to guide you.

*

DORIAN BROADWAY is a weaver of magic, worker of roots, teller of oracular tales, and devotee to the natural world. He adores adventure, craft medicine and magic with gratitude, and values engaging divination with fearless curiosity. Most of all he finds purpose in being bewitched by folklore, folk magic, and in the communion with 'the folk' of this realm and beyond.

Feral by Dorian Broadway

Know, Love, Trust

Diane Wilkes

Know thyself anew every day, every moment.

Question and answer.

Know why and for whom you read.

Love what you do.

Love what you are able to do.

Know what you can't.

Embrace that moment when you do what you thought you couldn't.

Eschew self-puffery and self-deflation.

Be a clear vessel, but not an empty head.

See the best possible outcome.

Face and address the worst possible outcome.

Never see what isn't there.

Some things will be woven together only in your unique vision. Express them fearlessly.

Mistrust flattery and baseless criticism.

Recognize both.

Add new arrows to your quiver.

Go deep deep deep.

Never ignore the obvious.

Own your strengths and weaknesses.

Emphasize the strengths.

Stretch those weaknesses into competency at the very least.

Read who people are as discerningly as you do the cards.

See the cards everywhere, including yourself.

The gut: Trust the cards. Trust yourself.

*

DIANE WILKES has been divining since she first obtained a copy of the Gypsy Witch Fortune Cards, almost 50 years ago. Creatrix of the Storyteller Tarot, the Jane Austen Tarot, and the Jane Austen Oracle. Tarot Passages webmistress. Empress of the Northeastern Tarot Conclave.

Shake It, Then Ink It

Aitzie Olaechea

Within the 64 Hexagrams lies the heart of the I-Ching.

Apart from answering questions, it can also inspire in creating talismanic calligraphy.

Ask the heart for a wish, be clear and concise as there is no room for ambiguity on the casting table.

There is also no room for attachments, nor expectations – only trust and confidence.

Shake and throw the coins six times to create a six-line pattern.

Today the I-Ching says 'earth over mountain.'

Open each line of the hexagram Song Dynasty style.

Follow the early and late heaven sequence.

If you get lost in heaven, the number code is: 9-4-3-8-2-7-6-1

Observe the form of the hexagram and decode its meaning.

'Earth over mountain': An earth Qi hexagram cast on a metal day.

At first sight, it looks strong and fabulous, but metal is dead on a hot summer's day, and earth is just being born in the summer season.

Therefore give your talisman strength by adding supportive elements.

Gather your four treasures and be inspired by the ancient masters: Bada Shanren, Kukai, Laozi.

Listen to the sounds of Om Mani Padme Hum, take a breath and listen. Calm the mind, open the heart and let it all go.

The present is all there is.

Grind the ink stick to a consistent paste, not too watery then add some J Herbin 1670, so it shines.

Dip your brush and slide it on the paper, top to bottom, then left to right at a ninety degree angle.

Once complete, charge it with an invocation: Arabic, Latin, Chinese, Sanskrit or English – whatever comes to mind will do.

Seal your wish by stamping the talisman with your name chop.

Breathe, smile and let it go. Keep it, gift it or burn it.

> Pixiu, the mythical dragon, says "Practice makes perfect so return to the casting table once the sun and the moon change positions".

*

AITZIE OLAECHEA is a practitioner of both I-Ching and cartomancy. She has studied the 64 Hexagrams with Grand Master Chan Kun Wah and uses I-Ching to help with decisions on property investments, relationship and health matters and much more. As a cartomancer, Aitzie primarily works with Tarot and Lenormand and is a member of the Aradia Academy working with Camelia Elias in her Nonreading program.

Open Heart by Aitzie Olaechea

To Read the Tarot

Annie Kaye

There is no rule except to be exquisitely alive to what is seen and unseen. Meantime, if you want advice on reading cards, why not ask the trumps?

Observe quickly, astutely. The cleverest one on the street keeps quiet among the hawkers. Seduction is part of the game.

So many complicated layers! Look beyond the writing. What you see flowers in silence.

Know the truth about agency. You have it. Meet its gaze.

You are sovereign here – you needn't even uncross your legs when the messengers arrive.

Don't throw tradition away. Learn from it. Let it mark your hands.

"Shoot me and put me out of my misery. Or, maybe not. I'm not sure." Treasure that exquisite squirming moment.

Sometimes you just need to go somewhere – the journey is more important than the destination. Still, might as well go in style.

To find the truth, tip the scales in favor of the lie. Honestly.

He who illuminates the past... illuminates the past.

Just like everybody else, you don't have a clue what's going on. Kind of a relief, isn't it? Now you can enjoy the ride.

Opening or closing the mouth of another is a powerful act. Why are you doing this? Are you sure?

Acquiesce to your utter helplessness. It no longer matters if you are traitor or martyr. This gives you a chance to be still.

Weed the garden. Talking heads are overrated and don't last.

Precision: Comb unruly thoughts till they flow straight and true. Keep to the topic. (Except when you don't.)

Sometimes you need to get all up in your stuff. Sometimes someone else needs to get all up in your stuff. It can be hard to tell the difference.

How glorious when the inner fire bursts through and connects with the source! It's usually inconvenient for the inhabitants, though.

When you pour out what is on the surface, you nourish what lies deep below. To do this well, it's preferable to be naked under the stars. (An outdoor café in shorts might be okay.)

As you catch a moon-drop on your tongue, the city reels away. Remember that the ground you rest on is built atop an ocean. You are held up by a crawfish.

Advice to a reader: When the sun sweats light, twin souls find one another.

You are not asked to assess, simply to announce. Do so, with fanfare and panache.

You are embedded in the story of the world. A new story lies beyond the mirror frame. So the question is...?

To read the Tarot, forget the previous rules. Walk forward.

*

ANNIE KAYE (Andrea Kiel) lives a magical life of cards, paint, mathematics, and incantation in the southern USA. She teaches trigonometry and calculus and edits the Math Poetry Sweat Shop Journal, a showcase for student poet-mathematicians. The Zen wheel is her art.

Don't Forget Your Cards

Robert Scott

Always have a pack of cards handy

When leaving the house, pick up cards, keys, wallet and hat.

If you can't read for yourself, you can't read for anyone else.

You don't have to read cards on a moment's notice, but be able to.

A pack of cards pairs well with strong coffee, or good wine.

Count the cards when getting a new pack, and before leaving a gig.

People aren't paying for your time, they are paying for an answer, and a story.

"Belief" is not required.

If you want to know the future, understand the present.

Don't keep your eyes on the cards so much that you don't look at the face of your client.

Talking about cards isn't the same as reading the cards.

Don't say it like carrot.

Unused packs are a waste.

It's possible to give a reading without giving a name or title of the card.

My father plays poker. I suppose cards run in the family.

A deck is a deck is a deck. Makes no difference.

The cards are both a museum and a library.

Every reader, at some point, probably ought to make a pack.

Take reading cards seriously, but not too seriously. Laugh, for fuck's sake.

You know you're magic when other people see it, and you are wearing "normal" clothes.

People talk shit about fortune-tellers, until they need one.

Everyone needs a little magic sometimes.

*

ROBERT SCOTT has regularly contributed to *The Carto-mancer* magazine, and has edited *The Diviner's Hand-book: Writings on Ancient and Modern Divination Practices* published by Bibliotheca Alexandrina. Robert reads cards, preaching about illusion, then killing it, and resides in Middletown, Ohio with his wife and dogs.

Entering The Majors' Ark

Joeanne Levister Mitchell

Make sure the reading table has four even legs, because once out on the waters of the Querent's unconscious cards can slide off the edge.

When sitting with the Querent, the Reader should never remove her veil. Keep your Mysteries to yourself.

There is always a bun in the oven. Every question contains an unspoken query as a core.

Never let the outer appearance of a Querent or their personality influence an interpretation.

Best to speak on what you see on the Table!

There is no need to filter or edit an incoming transmission.

Go straight ahead!

Remember every Querent has a blind spot.

Always have a stylized lamp, or candle on, or over your table.

Do not have a clock in the reading space. No tick, tick, tick. Do not wear a watch. Be creative as to determining the end of a session. Clocks are of the day–world and its routines.

Each layout is an enchantment, a formula for healing, a solution, and a map.

The Reader assumes the POV of the Hanging Man. Things are upside down. Don't get dizzy. (Or seasick.)

All manner of dead things will rise from the waters to whisper at the edges of the table. Listen!

The inner seeks to align itself with the outer. Showing the how of such an alignment is the purpose of divination and an Art.

Do not allow any projections or shadows released from the opened portal of the layout to take shelter in your physical or psychological space! Place mirrors or water bowls in view and use smoke or flower arrangements to protect your personal space.

The cards which have fallen have volunteered to tell this tale. Respect and honor their bravery.

Follow the shimmer. Look for the energy in the cards as it moves in the layout. It is your guide to interpretation in even the darkest places.

Keep both feet firmly on the floor to ground all the energies. Surges of defensive energy from the Querent are very counterproductive. Remain calm and gentle.

What is shown in the cards is what needed to be bought to light. This is an exchange and a service provided. Do not read for free!

You have entered the waters of the unconscious and braved Davy Jones' locker in the underworld of the Querent.

When the session is over, collect the cards on the table into a pile and STAND. See yourself leaving the watery realms and returning to dry land. The reading is over.

Or is it? Don't forget the Fool's Dog bites. Always follow up with your clients.

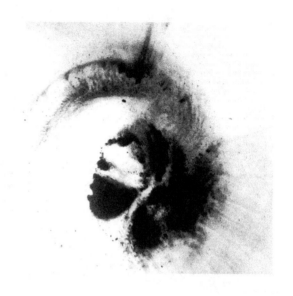

The Fortune-Teller by Camelia Elias

*

JOEANNE LEVISTER MITCHELL was born in the urban out-posts of Hoodoo culture in a suburb of New York City in the early 1950s. A card reader since the age of 12, lifelong student of occult sciences, who loves all manner of craftwork. She has blogged about cards, written poetry and prose as Mama Whodun at *Nocturnal Nuances.*

Cut See Voice

Miguel Marques

It all starts and ends with a question.

There is no beginning and no end: you enter at the first card, and exit at the last.

Everything you need to know is in the cards before you.

Whenever in doubt, remember: there are always more cards in that pile.

There is no polarity in Nature; Nature just is. It is we who create polarities by judging what we see. Any event has the potential to be exquisitely beautiful or excruciatingly soul-shattering.

If the heart is concerned, the reading will not be true. Then you will die.

Preoccupied with a single leaf, you will miss the tree; preoccupied with a single tree, you will miss the forest. Preoccupied with the forest, you will miss the leaf. See everything in its entirety . . . effortlessly.

Be aware of yourself. Accept yourself as you are.

Your eyes and voice are essential in documenting the reading.

The words must harmonize with the pictures. Follow the visual rhythm you see in the cards. No more, no less.

Search for the underlying meaning of each card in all readings, without ever losing sight of your context.

Ground your ideas; be practical.

Remove from your reading everything that is superfluous. Bring everything together in one place.

Remember your individuality, but keep your roots.

Let the wisdom you have developed through life allow you to see through any preconceived notions.

There is no path. There are several paths at any given time.

It is never about life or death. But it is always about life and, sometimes, it is also about death.

You are not paid to confirm whatever opinions the sitter has. You are being paid to believe in the cards.

You are not a mind reader. You are a card reader.

Sitters are very good at distracting. Be as keen-eyed as a lion.

Practice the mantra: Shuffle, deal, read! Shuffle, deal, read! Shuffle, deal, read! shuffle, deal, read; shuffle, deal, read! Shuffle, deal, read; shuffle, deal, read; shuffle, deal, read . . .

*

MIGUEL MARQUES once had a question: "How does the tarot work?" To find the answer, he set out to buy a deck and a book. He never did understand the book (even if in some weird metaphysical way it all made perfect sense in his head), but he understood comics and how pictures could be put together. And so, he kept on reading and has since never stopped.

Trumped Up Walk

Merete Veian

Lay out the cards, question in mind

Scan the cards

Be open

Prescribe a direction

Ask again

Determine a way

Run with it

Anticipate an outcome

Dig for answers

Revisit the question

Alterate the flow

Cut short

Eliminate distractions

Breathe

Ignore old habits

Crack the essence

Spark an idea

Formulate an answer

Assign a sentence

Say it out loud

Follow through

Walk on

*

MERETE VEIAN creates a body of work that reflects over walks through life. Where do we go, how do we feel, what's on our minds and what do we wish for? Mainly she works with fabrics. Paint, dye and stitch make up her creative palette to help her tell the stories. She reads cards and meditates with pen in hand, putting marks and words onto paper. The image here is hers.

Flying Völva

Erin Clark

When I reach for my deck, I am usually sprawled in bed, often naked. I always ask about love. I never ask, "Does he love me?" I assure you, he does. I just like to look in mirrors. I like to see myself in his eyes. Likewise, I just want to see myself in the cards.

I am currently the wandering Fool, and I don't care much about futures or fortunes or lists.

"I may have to miss this opportunity," I tell Camelia about being in her book.

"If you send me your words, I'll grace them with an ink artwork I made last night. What do you think of this one?" She texts, sending me an image, a clever seduction.

"It is mesmerizing," I say. "I feel like I'm flying when I look at it."

"It's a Völva with a drum, and a wand as an arrow, flying, of course."

Flying, like I literally do, paragliding in my wheelchair. A wand which is an arrow, like magic which finds its mark. The magic being mine, the mark being her book.

"I thought it was hands and a swirling penis. Also I have no idea what a Völva is," I say, considering her offering.

"A Völva is very good at swirling penises," she says, and I understand. She doesn't want lists from me, she wants my swirl.

She sends me a Wikipedia link. Völva: female shaman, Nordic.

"It sounds so much like vulva. So all the yin and yang is there," I say. It is certainly a worthy offer. Maybe I will give her what she wants.

"Historically speaking, every time a Völva was called to fix shit in times of crisis, and had to travel a long road, she'd demand to eat hearts and entrails, and sit on a raised throne made of 20 pillows, at least."

Of course, there is the fact of asking a favor of a woman who occupies a throne.

"That sounds perfectly reasonable." I say.

"That's what I always thought too. Then she would let a choir of enchanters carry her to her 'flying' spot."

Yes. I am about to travel a long road to the Andalucían mountains where I have a choir of Spanish babes who will carry me to my flying spot. The man I love will come and fly with me.

I am naked, sprawled in my bed. But I don't need the tarot to show me my image.

I am a swirl of ink artwork Camelia created last night.

*

ERIN CLARK: Writer. International Sex Icon. Currently lives in Spain.

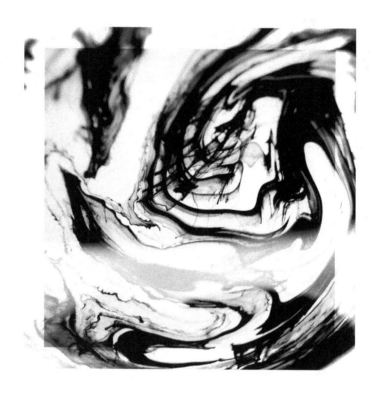

Völva by Camelia Elias

Ten-Chi-Jin

Camelia Elias

QUESTION. Is it me, a heavenly cause, or an earthly condition? What level are you on?

AGENCY. Who is doing what to whom? Lightning is a natural catastrophe, not your doing. If she cheats on you, pray to the heavens to strike her down.

TONE. The sky is high, the earth is low. Man whispers.

COLOR. What color is your flesh in the moonlight? Is the grass greener in the other's red cup?

LINE. All the way to heaven, or all the way to the belly of the earth? Straight or chopped? How can you tell if your eyes are crossed?

WEIGHT. Heavenly bodies are heavier than suited bodies. Suited bodies are heavier than naked bodies. Bones turn to dust, returning earth to heaven.

SIZE. A crowd makes everyone look small. Mankind's gossip is no match for the universe.

TENSION. Heaven can sit heavily on it, but a sharp iron blade can cut right through it.

STRETCH. Can you count the stars? No. Can you count the earth? Yes. One is one, ten is many. Your elastic, your breakpoint.

BALANCE. As above, so below. Either you see it, or you don't. 'A horse, a horse, my kingdom for a horse,' is just hysterical.

SPEED. Walking the earth takes time. In a dream, pursuing the heavenly dragons settles it in five seconds. Wheels with sticks in them will send you hanging.

SPACE. The sky is unlimited. The earth is up for grabs. The world of elevation is not the same as the under-world. When space is conquered, to whom does it belong?

FUNCTION. Natural or cultural? When the sun rises in the sky and the moon goes down below, what do you make of it? Truth is the job of justice.

VOICE. When the Angel's trumpet blows, all can hear it. The neighborhood gets busy reporting on the noise. But when the voices in your book are heavenly inspired, no one on earth needs to know about it.

RHYTHM. You don't get naked in winter. You don a heavy cloak and seek the caverns. Will you learn how to take hold of your mind? When summer comes, you seek the starry sky. When it's timely, the dogs will follow their nature, and howl at the moon.

RHYME. Three earthly beasts can mirror three ballooners. That's when you know that Cupid is human.

TEMPERAMENT. One hot, one cold, a short fuse, a long shot. Is it up or down? At the center or the margins? Red or black? Heaven only knows. What the heart knows, man doesn't always.

VARIETY. The Devil's many eyes see a blessing finger as a middle finger. The road to hell is paved with good intentions. Only a magician can invert the situation.

PROPORTION. Heaven makes it awesome. Earth tells you to shovel it and shut up.

EQUANIMITY. A question of fairness. Give unto Caesar and unto God. You call the shots on your positioning.

LUCK. When the cards are on the table, which give and which take? If the winner is not lucky, he won't take it all.

SUN TZU says: "All warfare is based on deception." Heaven is hell, hell is heaven. Read the damn cards.

*

CAMELIA ELIAS walks the path of Zen – sword in one hand, cards in the other.

Meet the Contributors

Each contribution in this book ends with a few lines describing the life and times of our authors.

Some provide their own art, or lend it to the contributions of others here.

One illustrator did not contribute words, but has graciously donated images of her artwork to this book. She introduces her art below.

You can read more about the contributors' work by contacting them or by following their websites, where relevant.

Authors

Dorian Broadway: dorianbroadway.com

Veronica Chamberlain: TarotwithV (FB page)

Cindie Chavez: cindiechavez.com

Sterling Clavelle: sterlingclavelle@gmail.com

Erin Clark: howtobeasexicon.com

Ryan Edward: www.inset.cards

Camelia Elias: cameliaelias.com

Enrique Enriquez: enrique.eenriquez@gmail.com

Natalia Forty: mistandether.com

Beverly Frable: beverly.tarotconnections (FB page)

Jane Green: janecartomancy.com

Wendy Lee Gadzuk: wendyleegadzuk.com

Yi-Sung Oliver Ho: oliverho.ca

Annie Kaye: andreakiel.com

Geoff Krueger: contrariandeterminism.com

Archie Leung: archiechleung@gmail.com

Miguel Marques: miguelmarques.me

Andrew Kyle McGregor: thehermitslamp.com

Joanne Levister Mitchell: mamawhodun.com

Aitzie Olaechea: aitzie.com

Devon Patel: @in_not_on (Instagram)

Markus Pfeil: http://portal.hs-weingarten.de/web/pfeilm

Rachel Pollack: rachelpollack.com

Caitriona Reed: fivechanges.com

Shelley Ruelle: sparrowtarot.com

Fortuna Sawahata: @Souldeepmagick (Instagram)

Debi Ann Scott: debimages@aol.com

Robert Scott: arcanaadvising.com

Simone Grace Seol: simonegraceseol.com

Jeff Silverstein: axiswave@gmail.com

Sherryl Smith: tarot-heritage.com

Bent Sørensen: aradiaacademy.com

Merete Veian: mereteveian.com

Charles Webb: cinemorphics.blogspot.com

James Wells: jameswells.wordpress.com

Diane Wilkes: tarotpassages.com

Adam Wolkoff: @honadam (Instagram)

ILLUSTRATOR

Michele Benzamin-Miki's statement:

My art, my work as an activist, performer, leadership-coach, my nearly four decades of teaching Zen, Hypnosis, Aikido and Iaido Sword – are intertwined into a single whole. I use sumi ink on paper, making visible an inner-sourced world of meditation and magical transformations, to allow the viewer to access a 'whole body state of being present.' Sometimes I return to add detailed realism in pencil or paint; sometimes I begin with an image I have already created. My art is an intersection between East and West, Realism and Abstraction, my Japanese/American heritage.

www.michelebenzaminmiki.com